She Dreams in Red is the story of journeys – from China to Canada, to Indonesia, to Mongolia into the mysteries of the human heart and romantic relationships.

Exploring the author's unique cultural background and history, travels and encounters with love and loss, these poems attempt to make sense of the world with simple images painted in clean brushstrokes.

D1364994

She Dreams in Red

Alexis Kienlen

Frontenac House
Calgary, Alberta

Book and cover design: Epix Design
Cover/Author photo: Natasha Kanji Photography

Library and Archives Canada Cataloguing in Publication

Kienlen, Alexis
       She dreams in red / Alexis Kienlen.

Poems.
ISBN 978-1-897181-12-6

      I. Title.

PS8621.I53S54 2007   C811'.6   C2007-900217-X

We acknowledge the support of the Canada Council for the Arts for our publishing program. We also acknowledge the support of The Alberta Foundation for the Arts.

Canada Council   Conseil des Arts
for the Arts   du Canada

Printed and bound in Canada
Published by Frontenac House Ltd.
1138 Frontenac Avenue S.W.
Calgary, Alberta, T2T 1B6, Canada
Tel: 403-245-2491 Fax: 403-245-2380
editor@frontenachouse.com   www.frontenachouse.com

For my parents

Acknowledgements

Special thanks to:

My teachers (especially Madeleine Dahlem), my writing groups and writing teachers (especially R. P. MacIntyre and McGinty Mondays), Jim Wong-Chu, the staff at *Ricepaper* magazine and everyone associated with the Asian Canadian Writers Workshop, the Canadian Cooperative Association for giving me the opportunity to go to Mongolia and Indonesia, libraries, writers and readers everywhere, my good friends who believed in me, everyone who hired me to write something for them, the Canadian Poetry Association, the Saskatchewan Writers Guild and all my family members.

Lastly, but most importantly, I'd like to thank Doreen and Cliff Kienlen for being the most supportive parents anyone could ever ask for.

Thank you for letting me be a dreamer, and thanks for helping me to have the courage and strength to chase those dreams.

A few words from my travels that appear in this book:
   bajai – A small mechanized Indonesian vehicle.
   boddhisattvas – A Buddhist term for enlightened beings who, out of compassion, forego nirvana in order to help others reach that state.
   Chinggis – The Mongolian name for Genghis Khan.
   ger – The Mongolian word for "yurt", a small hut used by the nomads.
   Halo (pronounced "hallow") – "Hello" in Indonesian.
   mala – A string of beads used for counting prayers in Hindu or Buddhist practice.

Contents

Mongolia

Tibet

Love and Lust

Chinese Café

chinese café

i want to eat chinese all the time
ivory chopsticks between my fingers,
porcelain bowls in my palms.

i want to sit on the red vinyl seats,
crack cookies between my canines,
floss my teeth with fortunes.

i love those old chinese cafés,
jasmine, chrysanthemum, or green tea.

i want to savour pork dumplings,
dribble hoisin, garlic and black bean sauce over rice,
want to twist and drip noodles into my mouth,
lick my lips.

i crave those wontons,
thrust my tongue deep in the custard tarts.

this chinese café stays open all night.

the boat

the boat looked big from the outside,
but inside, it was smaller than a womb.

crammed together in its dark depths,
amid the stench, fear and sadness,
they waited.

sometimes,
the boat shook like a drunken mother,
trying to free her children.

my grandfather crouched in the corners,
closed his eyes to avoid the sights,
dreamed of the new world,
tried not to listen to the sounds of others.

waited,
knowing he would be born again
on the shore.

society of bachelors

at night,
they lay under scratchy wool blankets,
shivered in cold damp
back rooms.

the only people who spoke the language
were men.

in cafés,
the men stole time in the booths,
whispered to each other,
leaned against walls,
searched for female faces.

their lonely fingers rolled cigarettes,
stared at nicotine-stained fingers,
dreamed of women waiting back home.

forgotten wife

my grandfather had another wife
before he met my grandmother
i picture his chinese wife
looking out the window
towards canada's cold waters
i see her waiting
for letters and cheques
she sits looking down at her tea leaves
wondering about the stranger
that she married

melfort café

she had never seen a man like him
before.
so serious and charming.
dark eyes with a mysterious slant,
creamy brown skin.

he thought she was the prettiest thing.
seventeen and rosy cheeked,
blue grey eyes and innocent skin.

the way she lifted her teacup made him forget,
about that woman in china.
made him think about her legs,
and what he would have to say,
to make her laugh,
make her leave
with him.

winks

1.
grandpa winked six times
they kept on arriving,
with asian eyes and white skins.

people said they had confusing faces.

mom said she was always confused.

she never knew why people were staring.

she never realized she had different cultures
stamped on her face.

2.
yellow china on white skin,
only single happiness.

(double happiness is still in asia)

in saskatoon

tablecloths for the restaurant

wonton soup
streets on the west side where the hookers walk

arrival of five girls with slant eyes

english names.

making half

1.

wives separated across the ocean.
you remember her chinese name,
forget the way her skin smells,
whether she has any birthmarks,
the sound of her voice.

second wife wants to believe
she is first.
the children don't know any different.

she is the one you share your bed with,
the one who reaches out,
holds your hand when the memories shake you awake.

2.

you look at your daughters
wonder how you created them.

you notice their features,
the way people see them,
turns them into others.

you look at your hands,
hold onto the brown skin of your husband's
hands.
he isn't married to you, but he's your husband anyway.

you have created six white chinese kids.
you always notice the stares,
the raised eyebrows,
the wondering.

near 20th street

eating rice out of bowls,
running back and forth between the restaurant,
the linen store,
her sisters holding medals,
my mother with her nose
in a fat russian novel.

running down the street late at night,
past the lurching rumble of city buses,
chinese grocery stores,
the movie theatre.
my mother ran as fast as
her dreams could go.

slant eyes chink

they called my mom this
these words marked my face
i kept my eyes closed to see better in the dark,
rice tastes better
when your eyes are closed.

words slapped my mother's face,
left blue marks on my ass.

separate dinners

she would cook
different dishes for the two parts
of the family.

chopsticks battled with forks
forks tried to grasp the chopsticks
but the wood was too thick and heavy,
they got stuck in the tines.
the children picked up the forks,
the father uses chopsticks,
pushes the fork onto the floor with a clatter,
children drink milk,
fill forks with macaroni and cheese,
smack their lips.

the father slurps up chinese cabbage,
bok choy, mushrooms,
holds his bowl close to his face,
uses chopsticks to scoop out the grains
of rice.
the mother hurries to the kitchen,
gets more water for tea,
eats vegetables soaked in oyster sauce,
a spoonful of macaroni,
she whisks the dishes away.
green bok choy,
white dishes,
yellow macaroni.

grandma's table

four children have gone,
and at this point, the two left
only want north american food.
grandma cooks in shifts.

chinese grandfather wants rice and bok choy,
every night, chopsticks and a bowl of tea
at his place setting.
my grandmother eats with him,
doesn't like a person to swallow food alone.

by the age of thirteen, my mother hates rice,
says it clings to her insides,
swears she'll never cook it in her own house.
she pushes it away from her,
reaches for the macaroni.

the secret

twenty-five years and no wedding ring,
sisters began to plan the party,
whispering behind hands.

when the mother hears,
she lies in bed crying,
holds her hair over her eyes.

one sister starts to suspect,
goes through drawers,
rummages through family history.
no wedding photos,
no stories of cake,
drunken relatives,
fragments of a wedding dress.

the mother keeps it inside,
swallows it with the rice
she cooks,
did not speak of the woman
hiding in the darkness.

wonton soup

feet dangling,
back of knees stuck to red vinyl booth.

always wonton soup,
buns filled with pink strips of bbq pork.

i stared around the room,
wondered if asia was in my eyes.

the funeral

family legend has it
i was a monster
the day of my grandfather's funeral.

i wore a red ribbon in my hair,
but i didn't go to the service.
instead, i stayed at home and screamed.

my grandmother wasn't allowed to go either,
she stayed home with me,
she didn't scream along,
but she may have wanted to.

chinese funeral

when my uncle dies
he is buried in an old chinatown of the cemetery.
the markers are large,
black with chinese script
running down the sides.

my mother recognizes
family names of children
she grew up with
lee, mack, tsang, wong, yee.

all the chinese patriarchs are here,
the first to come,
and those born here,
lined up in this neighbourhood,
wives off to the side.

we stand, looking at the gravestones,
bury our own ashes in the soil.

that night,
we will sip tea,
eat rice,
ginger beef and squid,
remember.

ancestor worship

rain in our faces
hard to hold onto umbrellas
while holding flowers.

standing with relatives
i've never met
i see your headstone for the first time
you've been dead for over 25 years.
i don't remember stretching my three-year-old
hand to meet yours,
but i believe the family mythology,
i was the only grandchild you held.

now here we are,
me in the rain with relatives,
you under the stones.
Beside me, your adopted son, his wife,
and their sons, my aunts, your daughters,
white chinese worshipping for the first time.

we place whiskey and chicken in front of your grave,
burn incense and bow three times to
sky, earth and below.
pour whiskey on the earth,
tear flesh from chicken,
throw the gnawed bones on the earth,
bow in the rain.
i want to understand
want to ask so many questions,
but you can't answer.
i can't open my mouth to speak the right language.
i say nothing,
bow in the rain.

robbery

i've stolen my mother's voice
hers is getting weaker,
mine gets louder all the time.

my mother has kidnapped my grandmother's skin,
hands and the way she clicks her tongue.

i too will raise my daughter to be a thief.

steam the rice

i love a man who knows,
a man who is not afraid to cut peppers
with a cleaver.
he fans them out over a cutting board,
like an abstract painting.

he slices cubes of tofu,
blends vegetables together,
throws them into a hot pan,
fries with skill,
and ease,
keeps smiling at me
he puts the stir fry on a platter,
rice into a bowl,
slides it toward me.
we both eat with chopsticks,
sweetly satisfied,
we cuddle on the couch,
get ready for dessert.

Indonesia

call to prayer

the call to prayer carries,
echoes through crooked little streets,
small mazes i don't understand,
past the children,
the older women cradling them
in batik slings,
bare feet and dusty smiles,
speaking those fast words,
i don't understand.

from my balcony,
i look out towards the mosques
tall towers
among squat little houses.

walking to work in indonesia

in indonesia, i walk to work
have to say "halo" to everyone i pass,
the old woman in the wheelchair,
sitting in the sun,
the other woman with tired hands
who wears her hair in two ponytails,
face covered with freckles.
there is a woman who always talks to me,
even though i can't understand her,
she balances her lazy-eyed child on her hip,
the young men sit on the corner in doorways
and giggle,
smile at me,
i love my neighbourhood,
the welcome i feel,
walking to work.

the night market

best of carnivals is
the night market,
blankets spread out.
everyone wants your money,
for sunglasses, pirated cds, sing karaoke,
fruit fresh from tree and, if you want, i'll crack
skin open for you.

do you speak indonesian, want to barter
i impress with halting bartering,
they think i don't understand the dance,
i think i do.

finally the woman selling mangoes yells loud enough,
catches my attention and i start the bartering dance
with three no,
two, no three, no one, okay two.

i walk off with two mangoes in a bag,
past the vendors,
noise, the smells,
carnival of it all.

under the scrutiny
of small eyes

small eyes stare,
follow my movements,
i am such a foreign woman.

in their eyes,
i am a harlot,
a woman on baywatch.
i probably have a lot of money,
and four cars.

halo mister, they say.
(this is the proper way to greet foreigners)

i can't understand anything else they say,
they can't understand me.
into the dark i slip,
keep watching.

swimming in indonesian waters

in my scandalous one-piece bathing suit,
the muslim women stare at my
bare shoulders.
i wonder if i should put on a t-shirt,
but i don't want to.
the women cover their shoulders,
some even wear shorts.
the children like the water better,
float and splash,
swim out to their grandpas.
the water becomes kid soup
as the children pour in,
jabber about
and stare at the foreign woman
across the water.

games in indonesia

the old men let me watch the game,
i don't understand it,
they speak in indonesian,
slap tiles onto the table,
hard and fast,
blow smoke in my face.

i keep looking at their teeth,
stained with nicotine,
their gap-toothed smiles,
slam the tiles down,
i jump at each bang.

one man keeps looking at me,
puts his arm around me,
squeezes and calls me his girlfriend.
i don't know about that,
so i shake him off,
leave them to slapping tiles,
make an excuse to go,
head off to that husband
i don't have.

talking in other countries

they think i am rude,
i try to talk but end up confusing.
try to explain, but the words circle round,
my words are too light,
they only evaporate on the air.

i try to speak less,
try to swallow my words.

i find that my words nourish me,
i build up a cellar inside myself,
digest the flavour
of my words.

call to prayer after the bomb

the wailing chant sounds,
washes over the streets,
men walk towards the mosques,
today i follow too.

it is four days
after the bombs exploded in bali,
i'm in jakarta,
far away but still close.

i try not to think about it,
the demon trapped
on the other side of the window,
fear knocks,
tries to get in.

i walk towards the mosque,
mind filled with images i've seen on tv
bodies torn apart
wreckage, rubble.

tonight there are only the men,
going to the mosque,
i slip through the shadows,
stand outside
watch outside as they pray,

sounds after the bomb

sounds after the attack
stayed the same,
men chanting,
noisy clatter of *bajais*
roar of motor scooters.
i watch the dusty dirty
street and the always grey sky.

there should be something different
after the explosion of a bomb,
some kind of silence,
some kind of halt.

but the truth is,
nothing stops.

love after the bomb

late in the night,
it shatters,
bodies break.
broken glass,
"this is where our children play"
parents repeat.
television is full of reports of destruction,
tears that fall somewhere between
night and ocean.

you have not been watching the news,
halfway across the world.
you don't understand

when you call,
you sound so far away,
i want to talk about the bomb,
but you drop your own.

you tell me you don't
love me any more,
my voice breaks,
somewhere between night and ocean,
i hang up,
begin to survey,
shattered glass, rubble,
the wreckage.

Mongolia

ancient land of mongolia

i trudge through desert,
choking on dust,
space more ancient than i can understand.

past carcasses that sink into the earth,
dirt that knows too much,
bones of animals.

the wisdom of this space
frightens me.
in this vastness i hear the murmurs of
earth's memories,
beating hooves,
warrior cries.

the age of the land threatens
my young heart,
steals me away,
dwarfs my youth,
frightens me into reverence.

on i walk through time and space.

sky worship

i lie on my back,
put my legs up,
walk across the sky,
the huge expanse
threatens to swallow me.

i am the safest
under a pure blue sky,
in the vastness of a blue desert,
that drives others to madness,
i am in an oasis.

sky envelopes you.
arms outstretched,
you pull fabric back from your fingers,
let the sand stream through.

mongolian cheeks

wind is a demon here
it batters and bruises
whips your face until your cheeks bleed,
i take my soft city fingers,
rub them across your cracked,
aged skin.

inside the *ger*

rotate the wheel,
thread the rope through the spokes,
stare at the canvas above your head,
marvel at the light that glistens
through the cracks,
the hint of sky that peeks into your home.

the wrist *mala*

beads circle my wrist,
i try to convince myself
that i am a buddhist,
try to believe the history,
know it deep inside my skin.

i am scared,
i am dishonest,
the yellow beads scream reality to my face,
ask me the truth.

top of the hill

from up here,
bones, rocks, fields around me,
mongolia is more ancient than time,
how many centuries of life have passed here,
how many people have ridden,
hunted, died here.

sky and stones are too wise,
they refuse to tell me,
let me know all that has happened here.

the communists attack

blue skies hid death,
when russians smashed the buddhas,
spat on *chinggis*,
the rest of the world was too far away,
screams too quiet,
sky too blue.

blood underneath

i can hear the chanting,
bells and horns,
sound comes up from the ground,
rises up from where they were buried.

when they killed them,
orange robes were stained with red,
red stained desert
soaked into plants.

cries were swallowed up
by rocks,
eaten by time,
i hear the distant echo,
in the faces of the golden buddhas
in the temples.

the ancient city

after miles of nothingness,
dust and blue sky.
the rubble rises out of space.

stones and broken buildings,
sign of the destruction of
the ancient city.
stones sit like fallen sin,
reminders that empires rise
and fall,
stories don't last forever.

we stand on ancient space,
dream of men on horses,
breathe history.

have a safe journey

before we leave the village,
he pulls a bottle of vodka from
the hidden pocket inside his coat.
he unscrews the cap and i think of russia
he pulls a small cup from his sleeve,
index finger in the shot glass,
flicks to the east, the west, the heavens,
touches his third eye.

there is no poison here,
only strong drink.
a sip clears sinuses.

it's all i can do not to shoot it back,
savour the good burning, the bite going down,
shot after shot.
harshness, dizziness for all but our driver.

he tucks the bottle away,
wishes us a good journey,
we stumble to the jeep,
drive off,
weaving,
bouncing across the worn ruts
in the desert.

Tibet

a prayer for tibet

1.
north wind spirits
fly with red cloaks
and angry hearts.

break our gods,
smash our temples,
split our families,
but they cannot cut our hearts.

they can't kill the dharma,
it is the stone of the universe.

all we do is walk on it,
all we do is walk.

trudging through
snow steel sleet
trudging toward the light,
flying towards forms,
hands outstretched
for a thread of rainbow.

2.
orange thread,
through my village,
through my heart.
my candle
threads through my lives,
my mother's lives,
my mother's mother's lives.

we all grab hold,
waiting for it to pull us out of
the cycle.

3.
we use the demons to chase away our fears,
we picture the rotting of our bodies,
the withering of our faces.

it never stops.

the cycles go on and on,
no one knows why.
we all wear the same face,
just different masks.

the hand that kills my brother,
the man that rapes my mother,
in my mind,
they belong to me.

they dance from my body,
like a six-armed demon,
i want to love them,
i have to love them.
it's the Way.

4.
the drums were not loud enough to warn us,
the horns were not long enough to catch the whispers,
our eyes were facing the wrong way.

we never envisioned this,
never saw the piles of bodies,
the burial cloaks of the monks.

one person may have been listening
meditating
a holy man
could have tasted the blood in the air,
but kept quiet about it.

but we were not ready for
the guns in our palace,
the death in our streets,
the cries in the dark.

5.

i'm counting the beads on my *mala*,
consulting oracles,
praying to the buddhas
and the *bodhisattvas*.

but i can't understand the answers,
i speak to the world,
i speak to myself
i conserve my strength
and don't mark down the differences.

i don't understand now,
but liberation will be received eventually.

6.
red from the blood,
not the robes.

thousands pray.
a spectacled god child
forced to flee.

people wandering through mountains
and dust,
chewing on the dirt in their mouths,
only to rise again,
keep walking.

a quiet sounding of trumpets,
a gentle ringing of bells,
the light of bells,
the light of sky,
air, earth.

the eyes of truth,
a hand, calm,
the gentle lull.

Love and Lust

she dreams in red

she dreams in red fire
red feelings in a green world
she holds the axe over her head
blood splashes like candle wax onto her feet
she dreams of warmth
full-fledged fire against her face
she dreams of embracing love
secrets kept in scarlet rooms
bright red lipstick to make her famous
fire engines scream through
dark nights
love lit traffic lights
she dreams of being attacked by vampires
bleeding red roses
cherries in her hair
exclamations of red upon her mouth
she holds the apples
sprays the blood
drops the roses

the girl in front

the girl in front of you
has a red ponytail.
you write love poems,
mouth them to the back of her neck,
you'd like her to turn around,
but she doesn't know how you feel.
if she did,
she probably wouldn't care.
you think of her in ways
that blow your sixteen-year-old mind,
and make you do your own laundry.
you tattoo eyes of desire
into her back.

she doesn't move,
but you swear
her ponytail says
yes.

old fashioned farm love

remember when you picked me up
in that red ford truck,
and we drove up and down the back roads,
playing the radio real loud.

i liked to sit in the middle,
so i could be closer to you.

if we were both feeling good,
we'd find a nice field
and park the truck,
and lie in the back
on that scratchy blanket you kept
on your truck seat.
we'd look at the stars,
slide closer to each other.

after some kissing,
my fingers would wrestle with the belt
on your jeans.

you'd be struggling with my bra.

finally we'd be naked,
the cool hotness of our skin would slide together.
the air was cool,
but our bodies kept us warm.

i loved looking at you,
as you came
the stars glimmered over your head.

we'd lie there for a couple minutes,
quiet.

struggle
then we'd get back in the truck,
you'd drive me back to my parent's house,
go back to yours.

you always made sure to
call me on monday.

that summer

it was too hot
grasshoppers arrived like plague,
devoured the crops.

and you, not knowing what you wanted,
cool lemonade that we could never drink fast enough.
ice cubes melted and watered down
the taste.

you came into my bedroom,
forgetting time and smelling of cigarette smoke,
other people at the late night bar.

you'd stick your chewing gum on my windowsill,
over the holes in my screen,
as you slid into my sheets,
tried to keep mosquitoes from my sleeping skin.

ideal tattoos

my ideal tattoos are ones
that i have earned

the laughlines at the corner of my mouth,
the freckle on my cheek,
my scars and scrapes,
the bruises you bite into my neck.

my favourite is the tear inside,
the mark you left when you borrowed
my virginity.

exclamations of red
upon her mouth

juice of peach runs down my chin
sticks to my lips
i bite into the soft ripe warm
pulp of the fruit
lick the deep hard pit
sweetness taints my mouth
juice runs
down
my hand
coating it
in the peach's
sweet sex

strawberry
drips off the plant,
red round raunchiness.
when you pluck a strawberry,
it sounds like hungry lips brushing
licking nipple,
indecent strawberry
growing on the underside of leaves.

orange mango wetness
draws me into warmth,
tongue a sliver in the expanse of mouth,
a flash of orange in a quiet room.
i love how your musician hands
peel back skin,
split me open,
make fluorescent insides overflow.

autumn river walk

we slip through the undergrowth
near the river
branches slap you in the face
but i duck underneath
outsmarting nature
your shoes crunch through the leaves
thrown like discarded fabric
from the great tattered cloaks
of the trees
the sounds of the city
are lost
only the stark telephone wires
speak of civilization
surrounded by the aroma
of the earth
i stop to look back at you
and notice shredded bits of leaves
glistening in your hair
like jewels on
oberon's crown

rain kisses

sweet droplets on your face
i long to kiss you in the rain
your hair brushes against
my face
clean green lapping seaweed
pink earthworms form
engagement rings
around my fingers
i like to kiss you in the rain
water droplets fly into our joining mouths
slip between my teeth

the poets

old man poets
stretch out their ink-stained fingers
exhale breath from nicotine-stained lungs,
and strain their eyes toward the young woman poets.
sitting across from them,
wide-eyed,
skin new
their hands have no callouses
free from ink smudges left on them from bad love,
broken poetic hearts.

skin on skin

i lie in bed with you,
white quilt over our brown skin
covers and comforts me.
i love the starkness of the room,
quiet zen of your space,
intertwined with the city street noises outside,
white walls and a chinese character
over my head,
your arms around me,
legs twined together,
hair splayed across
pillows, sheet, on skin
on skin.

you in blue

light filters in,
you are surrounded by blue,
soft in light,
curly hair waves
sit electric against your breasts.

i move towards you,
engulf myself in your paleness.

you wrap
warm arms around me.

we fall together,
lie down.

in the morning,
i am so full of woman,
that i start bleeding,
you give me silk scarves,
smile over the top
of your coffee mug.

i slip my underpants
in my back pocket,
sneak out the front door.

don't turn to wave,
just remember
you in blue.

silk scarf

i wish you had wound it,
over my body,
rubbed its softness,
over your breasts,
down into wet
sweetness, between your legs.

i wish
we'd played with it before,
run it over ourselves,
and around the room,
pulled it out of sleeves,
across skin,
done magic tricks with it.

i wish we'd nestled it
between us,
that you'd held it in your hand,
as we were touching.

i wish the silk scarf you'd given me,
smelled like our night
together.

join together

when we come together,
we bend and you lose your boy body,
grow hips and breasts
and i take yours
grow a penis
with you inside me.
my chest grows broader,
expands,
the movement changes us,
my voice deepens,
yours rises,
there is softness, heat and wet,
no knowing where one ends,
the other begins.

treasure hunting

you trace the plains of
my face
i am the prairies
your fingers drag in the rivers
formed by my expression
and brush against my eyelids
like a butterfly kiss
you rest a finger on my mouth
to remind me
to keep silent during the ritual
your fingers are looking
for something in me
you resume your search
wearing the tracks of your fingers
into my skin

cooking truth

you asked for the truth,
so i prepared it for you,
baked it and braised it,
garnished it with parsley,
served it to you on a black china plate.

you ate it all
but weren't satisfied,
you wanted more sugar,
more salt,
more something
but my capabilities only go so far.
there's nothing i can do to please your palate,
nothing i can do
to change
the bitter taste in your mouth.

dance of intimacy

i drive through the dark from your house
it's too late for sane people to be up
the windshield wipers dance forward like you and i
as i step forward
you retreat
as you lean to kiss me
i turn my head away
we're at the point
of never quite touching
we keep on dancing away from love
brushing away intimacy
in the same way
windshield wipers
scatter raindrops

distance between us

the distance between us
is roads wide
i slide onto my bed,
think of you,
wish i could sleep curled up
in the small of your back,
listen to your calm breathing.

when you and i are apart
in the same country,
the distance is greater.
the heat and tropics shrink
the distance.

still, i think about you,
wonder what you are doing,
wish i could trace the baby
beginnings of lines on your face.

erasing me

you're trying to wash away
the stains i've made in your life
you scrub your sheets to get rid of my smell
throw my cds and pictures into a drawer in your desk
toss my yogurt in the trash
pour my shampoo down the sink
you move your car seat back from where i've placed it
you think you've erased everything
until
one night
you're in the video store
a girl walks by
you catch a whiff of my perfume
and you remember

barren

my land has gone bad.
nothing will ever grow here.
everything's dried up and dead.

your voice is tired and dusty,
you take off your hat, cough,
spit,
then walk off.

i stand in the cold,
"come back," i say.
"grow."

lust blues

my body has retreated,
gone back into itself.
no one touches it any more.

it is starting to dry up,
wither.
i stand by the window,
let sun touch me,
lean towards strangers,
try to bump against them,
get some contact,
try to make something stir.

my body is lonely
i wear loose pajamas
you could slip them off
slide your hand under my shirt
i can't sleep
my bed is a barren desert
i pace back and forth
i flick the light on and off
lie down and rub my fingers over my body

then stop

absorb the memories that rest on my skin

the name on your back

you told me tattoos were holy,
slowly i am starting to believe.

you said you would never get someone else's
name written on you, only your own name.
(it makes it mine, you said)

you took off your clothes
to show them to me,
i loved those marks,
the scars between your breasts,
inscribed over your ass
(this is my name, you said.)

in all languages,
it means the same thing.

past histories

you lie in my arms like mark anthony
the snake is alive
she slides from the dark
slithers over my stomach
she drives stabbing fingernails into my nipples
he springs from my head fully armed
rakes his spear over your ribs
you lean to kiss me
his hair brushes my neck
i'm outlining my eyes with kohl
you ask why i'm laughing
i'm thinking of caesar
there's too much history here
too many bodies in the bed

i can't tell you how much
i miss you

I tell you too much.
About how I miss your hands your breath
the warmth of your chest your hipbones when they poke me
in the side, sex in all forms, your head between my legs,
someone to hold me, fulfillment, conquest, skin, limbs from
all sides and the sound and scent of desire.

I can't tell you how much I miss you any more.

your goddess

i want to be your goddess.
i want to rise,
white limbed,
many armed from your bed.
i'll speak with a forked tongue
that kisses and bruises.
i will be the jewel of your desire,
the one whose name you whisper
before you sleep.

you would suckle at my breast,
find birth and death in my arms.

give me the same reverence
as the woman of many names.

Alexis Kienlen is originally from Saskatoon, Saskatchewan. She is of mixed ethnic heritage: Chinese, French, German, and English/Scottish. She holds an International Studies degree from the University of Saskatchewan, and a Graduate Diploma in Journalism from Concordia University. Alexis has lived in Montreal, Wainwright Alberta, Grande Prairie Alberta, Vancouver, Indonesia and Mongolia. Her poetry, fiction and journalism pieces have appeared in numerous publications throughout Canada.